TopGear

Mad Cars

TopGe

BBC Children's Books
Published by the Penguin Group
Penguin Books Ltd, 80 Strand, London WC2R 0RL, England
Penguin Group (Australia) Ltd, 250 Camberwell Road,
Camberwell, Victoria 3124, Australia (a division of Pearson
Australia Group Pty Ltd)
Canada, India, New Zealand, South Africa

Published by BBC Children's Books, 2009
Text and design © Children's Character Books, 2009

10 9 8 7 6 5 4 3 2 1

Written by Jonathan Empson

ISBN: 978-1-40590-541-1
Printed in China

It's possibly the most **amazing**, maybe the **fastest** and almost certainly the **scariest** car ever made.

Contents

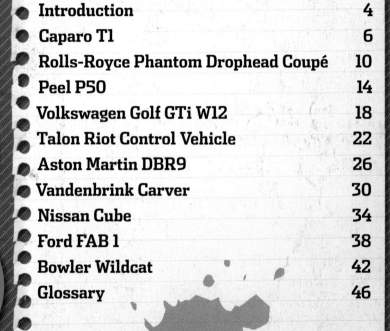

That's the **most fun** I've **ever** had in a car.

Very, **very** cool.

Introduction

Welcome to Top Gear Mad Cars!

Clarkson driving the Caparo T1

Brace yourself. The cars you're about to experience in the following pages are the work of some very strange minds. They are, in short, mad. Which is just as well, because this book is called Mad Cars, so if it was jam-packed with sensible family Toyotas and Volvos, you'd be quite disappointed.

Luckily, it isn't. We've selected some of the oddest cars featured on Top Gear and gathered them together safely in the pages of this book, where they can't hurt anyone.

Now then: these cars may all be a bit loopy, but they're deranged in different ways. Some are simply one wheel short of the full complement, like the Peel or the Vandenbrink. Some are insanely expensive, like the Rolls. Some are so over-the-top, you'd only

expect to see them in the cinema (as in on the screen, not in the back row eating popcorn). Some aren't even cars: the Talon's a riot-control lorry and it's only here because it forced its way in. And some of the cars are mad in an extremely high-speed way. Actually, that covers most of them.

But what all of these vehicles show us is what's possible when designers think outside the square. Or, in the case of the Cube, what's possible when they only think *in* squares. The cars may not be everyone's cup of tea, but the motoring world would be a more boring place without them – and Top Gear episodes would be a lot shorter.

TO INSANITY AND BEYOND!

Caparo T1

Sure, it looks like a Formula 1 car, but you can use it on the road. How mad is that? Well, very, as it happens. No-one's tried to do this before. Weight-for-weight, it's twice as powerful as a Bugatti Veyron. It accelerates so hard, any driver with an 'outie' tummy button will have an 'innie' by the time he hits 100mph. Which will be in 5 seconds.

You can **forget Enzos**, forget **Koenigseggs**: this is in a **different** league.

Remarkable-looking thing, isn't it?

VRROOMM

Top Gear Test

The Caparo T1 once caught fire at 150 mph so Jeremy Clarkson was a bit nervous on his test drive. Luckily he had a safety team on hand big enough to deal with a medium-sized plane crash. And he wore a flame-proof racing suit, so that 'if something goes wrong, all my organs will be held together in one big fireproof bag and they'll be easier to collect'. The floor came adrift and there was a fuel problem, and he kept spinning it – you have to drive really fast to get round corners, strangely – but Jeremy survived. And he liked it.

Why it's Mad

Spoiler:
So low, if you drive over a slice of toast, you'll scrape off the marmalade.

Brakes:
You couldn't stop more quickly if you ran into a tree.

Engine:
So much power, you'll get wheelspin in 4th gear.

Lights:
By the time you see where you're going, it's too late.

Roof:
To muffle your screams.

Wing:
Generates so much downforce, you could drive a T1 on the ceiling. If you have a really long ceiling, obviously.

How to Use

1. Fold yourself into the tight cockpit.
2. Attach the steering wheel (make sure it's the right way up).
3. Fasten safety harness.
4. Arm the fire extinguisher.
5. Turn on the master switch.
6. Put in your earplugs.
7. Write your will.
8. Fire up the engine.

This is **acceleration** like I have **never**, ever experienced.

Stats

Engine: 3.5-litre V8

Power: 575bhp

Top speed: 205mph

0-60mph: 2.5s

Weight: 550kg

Top Gear lap time: 1m 10.6s

Danger rating: 9/10

Rolls-Royce Phantom Drophead Coupé

'Drophead' just means 'convertible', but the heads of a few passers-by might actually come unscrewed and drop off as they crane their necks for a look at this fantastic machine. It's an exclusive version of one of the most exclusive cars in the world – it costs £50,000 more than the hard-top coupé. For your money you get an extra 460ft of body welding and a folding roof lined with cashmere, which is a kind of goat hair. Because of this car, many goats are now catching their deaths of cold.

James drove this 18ft-long, 2.6-tonne giant from the top of an aircraft carrier to the centre of London. An unusual test route, but that's what you get when James reads the maps. He arrived in London after dark, so as not to attract too much attention, but then decided he really liked being seen in it after all: 'I think this might be the coolest car in the world.'

> I believe deep in my heart that I look **good** in it. It's stylish and **contemporary.**

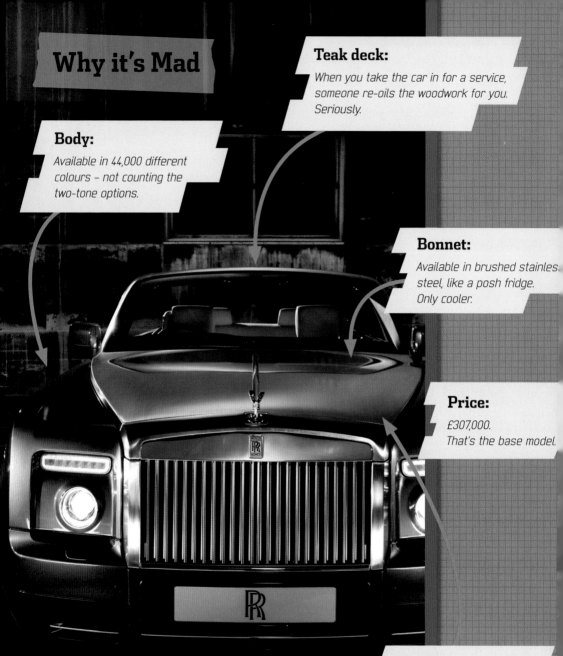

Why it's Mad

Teak deck:
When you take the car in for a service, someone re-oils the woodwork for you. Seriously.

Body:
Available in 44,000 different colours – not counting the two-tone options.

Bonnet:
Available in brushed stainles. steel, like a posh fridge. Only cooler.

Price:
£307,000.
That's the base model.

Engine:
6.75 litre V12 – so big, your granny could live inside it.

How to Use

1. Be very, very rich.
2. Don't be shy about it.
3. Sack your chauffeur:
   you'll want to drive this one yourself.

A **proper**
Rolls-Royce:
wonderful to drive,
beautifully made.

It's **exquisite**.

Stats

 Engine: 6.75-litre V12

 Power: 453bhp

 Top speed: 149mph (limited)

 0-60mph: 5.6s

 Weight: 2620kg

 Danger rating: 2/10

P IP

If you look at a Smart Fortwo and think 'I don't need all that raw power or interior space', the one-seater Peel P50 is for you. This model was built on the Isle of Man in the 1960s, cost under £200 new and it's the smallest production car ever made. It's only 54in long and 41in wide. No garage? No problem - just park it in the cupboard under the stairs.

Top Gear Test

Richard Hammond once voted the Peel as one of the Top 5 Worst Cars of All Time. Which is cruel – Richard should pick on a car his own size. Jeremy decided to find out for himself by driving a Peel P50 to work through London. Trouble is, Jeremy isn't small: he's 6ft 5in – that's 77in tall and the car, remember, is only 54in long. But by folding himself in places the human body is not meant to fold, Jeremy squeezed himself inside. Performance from the 49cc moped engine was feeble – but hey, it does 100mpg and, as a tricycle, it's exempt from London's Congestion Charge. When Jeremy got to work, he drove it right into his office at the BBC. The car's so tiny, it even fits into a lift.

Why it's Mad

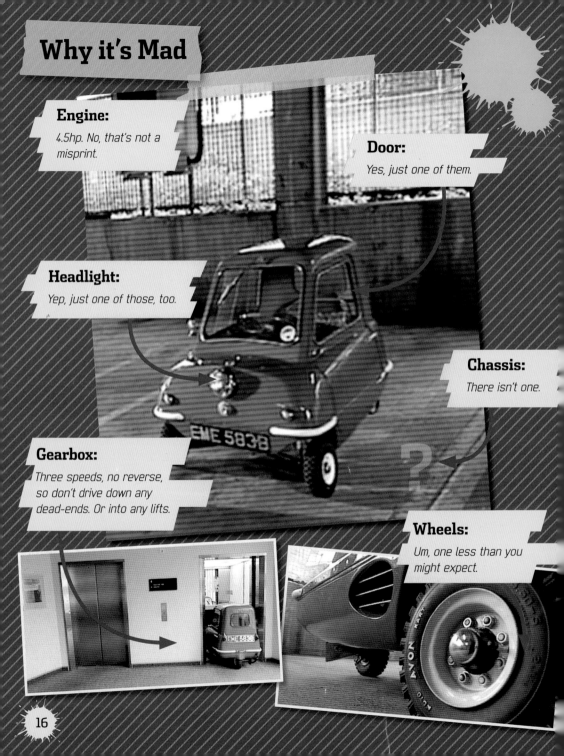

Engine:
4.5hp. No, that's not a misprint.

Door:
Yes, just one of them.

Headlight:
Yep, just one of those, too.

Chassis:
There isn't one.

Gearbox:
Three speeds, no reverse, so don't drive down any dead-ends. Or into any lifts.

Wheels:
Um, one less than you might expect.

EME 5838

How to Use

1. Take out life insurance –
   a bus driver might run you over and not
   even notice. So might a cyclist.
2. Go to the loo, empty pockets of all loose
   change etc to save weight.
3. Place one leg into footwell, then follow
   with rest of body.
4. Allow plenty of time for your journey –
   the top speed's 38mph.

The **best** car
we've ever had on
Top Gear.

It's the **ultimate**
in personal
mobility.

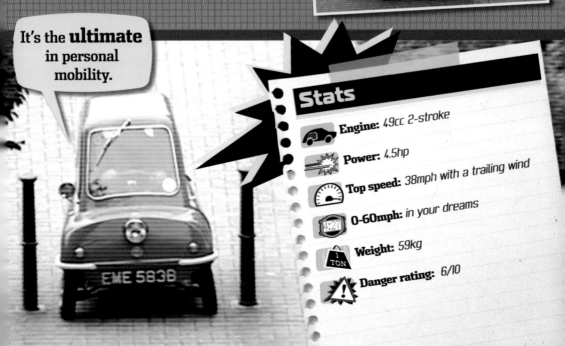

Stats

- **Engine:** 49cc 2-stroke
- **Power:** 4.5hp
- **Top speed:** 38mph with a trailing wind
- **0-60mph:** in your dreams
- **Weight:** 59kg
- **Danger rating:** 6/10

Volkswagon Golf
GTi W12

Volkswagon had to throw a concept car together in the space of eight weeks. So they took the rear axle and brakes from a Lamborghini Gallardo, the twin-turbo W12 engine from a Bentley Continental and a chunk of the back of an Audi R8 and shoehorned all these bits into the body of a Golf. Don't ask why. The GTi W12 is 6in wider and 3in lower than a normal Golf, and has an engine where the back-seat passengers normally sit.

Top Gear Test

Jeremy took the GTi W12 out onto the track and quickly discovered that most of the dashboard controls didn't actually work. But the engine did and the car was an absolute screamer in a straight line. Trouble is, it wasn't too happy going round corners. With all that power going to the rear wheels, it kept spinning, so it wasn't the fastest thing ever to go round the Top Gear test track. Jeremy's conclusion: 'If you want a slow car that looks like a Golf, get a Golf.'

It is an **insane** car, this!

19

Why it's Mad

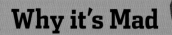

Roof:
Made of carbon fibre.

Wheelarches:
Flares add 6in to the normal Golf width...

Ride height:
...and it's 3in lower

Tyres:
Hard to spot, but they're there.

Brakes & suspension:
Um, not quite finished yet.

Engine:
641hp – over 8 times the power of a base-model Golf and 8 times as loud, too.

WOB : PS 650

How to Use

1. Steal it from VW
   (there's only one of them in existence).
2. Dress for hot weather
   (the fan and air-con don't work).
3. If you're planning on using the sat-nav,
   make sure you understand German.
4. Choose roads without any corners.

You **think** it's a Golf... but it **SO** isn't!

SKREEEEEEEEEEE

#*%*#!!

Stats

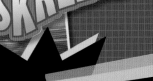 **Engine:** 6-litre W12 twin turbo

 Power: 641hp

 Top speed: 202mph

 0-60mph: 3.5s

 Top Gear lap time: 1m 29.6s

 Danger rating: 8/10

Talon Riot Control Vehicle

This is the vehicle that makes a Hummer look a bit puny. And cheap: this will set you back half a million quid. But if you've got to get the school team to a fixture on the other side of Baghdad, you might want to invest in a Talon. It takes 14 people, it's armour-plated to withstand gunfire, and it has a water cannon and grenade launcher so you can shoot back. Any dog who tries cocking his leg against its wheels is literally in for a nasty shock – the body's electrified with 20,000 volts. Passengers needn't worry about being caught short, though, there's a loo on board.

Top Gear Test

> If things get really **nasty** I can always just **head-butt** stuff.

This is not really a vehicle for beating the Top Gear power board lap record in, so Richard limited his test to dispersing some demonstrators with the water cannon, then driving through a Portacabin.

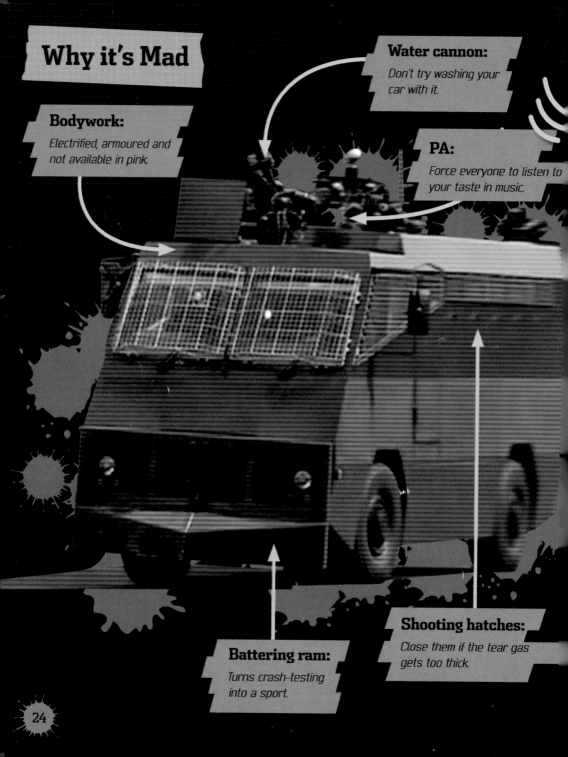

Why it's Mad

Water cannon:
Don't try washing your car with it.

Bodywork:
Electrified, armoured and not available in pink.

PA:
Force everyone to listen to your taste in music.

Battering ram:
Turns crash-testing into a sport.

Shooting hatches:
Close them if the tear gas gets too thick.

24

How to Use

1. Find an angry crowd to disperse. If you can't find one, try squirting random people in the town centre with the water cannon.
   That should make them angry.

2. Zap a few people with the electrified bodywork, and ram a few cars.

3. Plead guilty when your case comes to court and hope for a lenient sentence.

Grenade launcher.
Impulse generator.
Lovely.

Stats

Engine: 8.1-litre turbo diesel

Power: 205hp

Top speed: 65mph

Danger rating: 1/10

Aston Martin DBR9

This 600hp full-monty endurance racer is the perfect car in which to pop down to the shops if they're 1000 miles away and you're really, really desperate for that packet of cornflakes. Or it would be, if you could buy it, but you can't. You might be able to pick up a second-hand one for about half a million quid, but otherwise you'll have to make do with its little brother, the 550hp DBRS9, which is a snip at £175,000.

Top Gear Test

The Stig took this around the Top Gear track, and you could tell he was grinning behind his visor. OK, you couldn't really – no-one's quite sure if The Stig has a mouth to smile with. But he was about 10 seconds faster round the track than anything else.

Why it's Mad

Body:
Carbon-fibre panels. If there was any more carbon in it, it would be coal.

Noise:
Loud. Once you've heard this, you'll never hear anything again.

Air-con:
Yep, it's a racing car with climate control. Crazy.

ASTON MARTIN RACING

DBR9

59

Weight:
Twice the power-to-weight ratio of a DB9 – which is no shopping trolley.

Price:
Not available in shops.

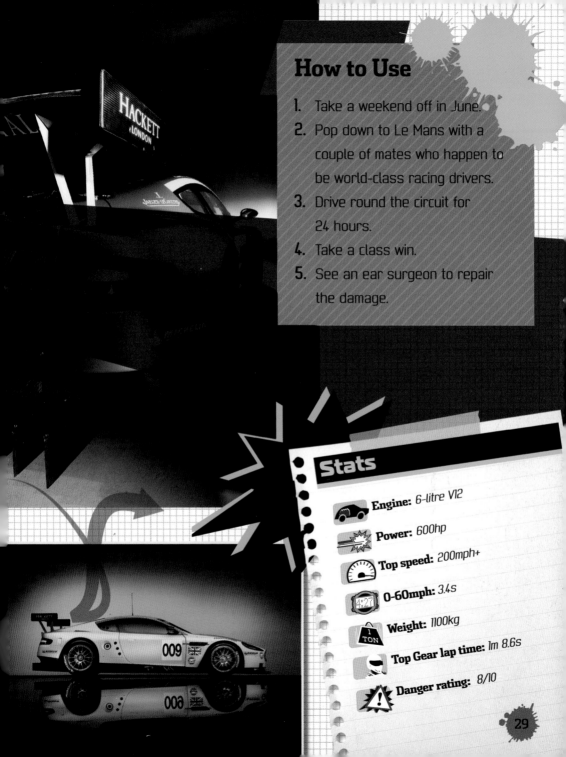

How to Use

1. Take a weekend off in June.
2. Pop down to Le Mans with a couple of mates who happen to be world-class racing drivers.
3. Drive round the circuit for 24 hours.
4. Take a class win.
5. See an ear surgeon to repair the damage.

Stats

Engine: 6-litre V12

Power: 600hp

Top speed: 200mph+

0-60mph: 3.4s

Weight: 1100kg

Top Gear lap time: 1m 8.6s

Danger rating: 8/10

Vandenbrink Carver

I've **never** had so much **fun** in a car.

It took 11 years to develop. It's expensive. The engine's tiny. It only carries two people and it's not very fast. But for £22,500, you'd at least expect to get four wheels, wouldn't you? Well, tough. The Carver only has three, because it's more like a car with a motorbike grafted onto the front. But like a bike, and like no other car, it tilts into corners.

Top Gear Test

Richard took this crazy Dutch invention for a spin – or should that be a lean – and you couldn't wipe the smile off his face. The quicker you turn the wheel, the more it leans – it's completely wild and enormous fun. It's almost like the thrill of riding a motorbike, only you don't need a helmet or strange leather clothing, you don't get wet when it rains and insects don't commit suicide in your face at 100mph. And Jeremy proved that the back seat was just about big enough for him to climb into – but much harder to climb out of again.

It's **insane!**

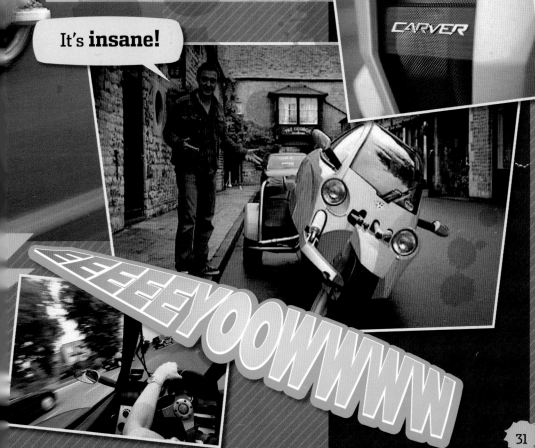

CARVER

EEEEEYOOWWWWW

Why it's Mad

Roof:
Look, it's even a convertible!

Lean:
Tilts to 45 degrees.
Watch out for
grazed elbows.

Engine:
45mpg – from a
car this mad!

Front suspension:
More girders than the Forth Bridge.

Wheels:
It's just so NOT a Reliant Robin.

How to Use

1. Hide the keys. Everyone will want a drive.
2. In fact, if you have more than one friend, ditch them.
3. In fact, if you have any luggage to carry, ditch that last friend, too.
4. Be warned: other cars will feel so ordinary after this.

The **gadget** to **end** all gadgets.

Stats

 Engine: 659cc turbocharged 4-cylinder

 Power: 68hp

 Top speed: 115mph

 0-60mph: 8.2s

 Weight: 643kg

 Danger rating: 4/10

Nissan Cube

This was the bestselling car in Japan a couple of years ago. It's also probably the squarest car ever made. That means it's not very exciting to look at. But if you wanted to give it to someone as a present, at least it would be easy to wrap.

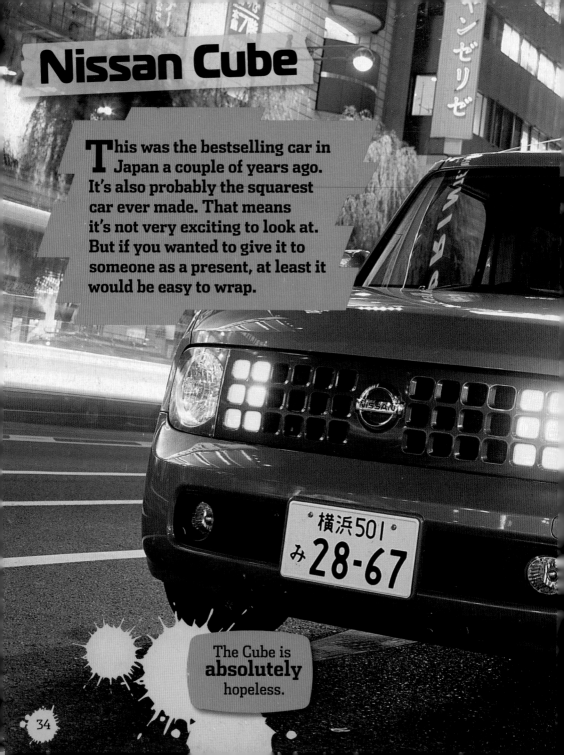

The Cube is **absolutely** hopeless.

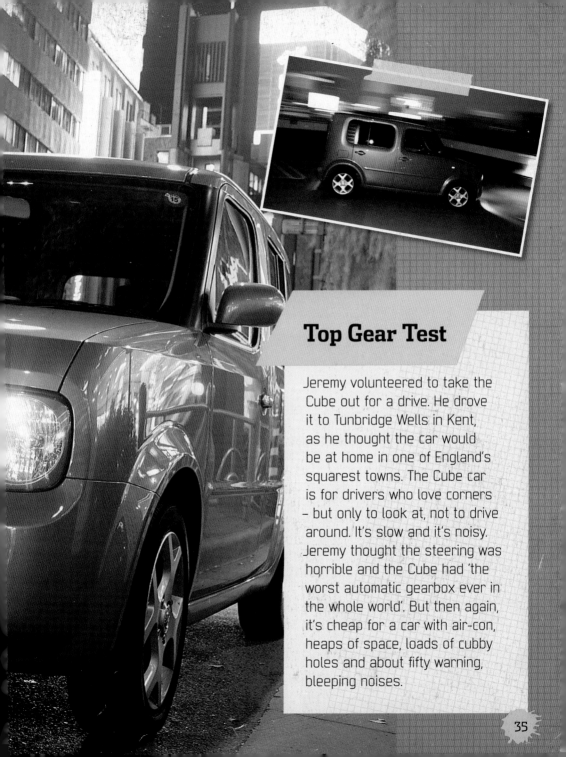

Top Gear Test

Jeremy volunteered to take the Cube out for a drive. He drove it to Tunbridge Wells in Kent, as he thought the car would be at home in one of England's squarest towns. The Cube car is for drivers who love corners – but only to look at, not to drive around. It's slow and it's noisy. Jeremy thought the steering was horrible and the Cube had 'the worst automatic gearbox ever in the whole world'. But then again, it's cheap for a car with air-con, heaps of space, loads of cubby holes and about fifty warning, bleeping noises.

Why it's Mad

Asymmetry:
That means the left side's different from the right. Like your hair after your mum's had a go at it.

Engine:
Completely square. Square valves, square pistons, the lot... actually, that's not true. It's a plain old Nissan Micra engine.

Shape:
It's really very square, isn't it? Apart from the wheels. They're quite round.

Rear engine:
Yep, it's also available with an extra electric motor to drive the rear wheels. Good idea – the front engine needs all the help it can get.

How to Use

1. Be square. Literally.
2. Being Japanese also helps.
3. Before you let your friends see you in it, make sure they know you value quirky styling above almost everything else, including performance.

Not at all **scary.**

Stats

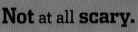

Engine: 1400cc 4-cylinder

Power: 97hp

Top speed: 103mph

0-60mph: 13s

Weight: 1150kg

Danger rating: 5/10 (only because you might fall asleep at the wheel, due to boredom)

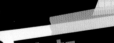

Ford FAB 1

In ancient times (the 1960s) there was a TV show called Thunderbirds. It was a bit like James Bond only with puppets and wobbly models to save money on actors and special effects. In 2004 it got made into a film with real actors – but they weren't as good as the puppets. And in the original series, aristocrat/secret agent Lady Penelope is chauffeured around in a pink, six-wheeled Rolls-Royce with the registration FAB 1. In the film, however, she drives this thing: a not-quite-as-fab Ford.

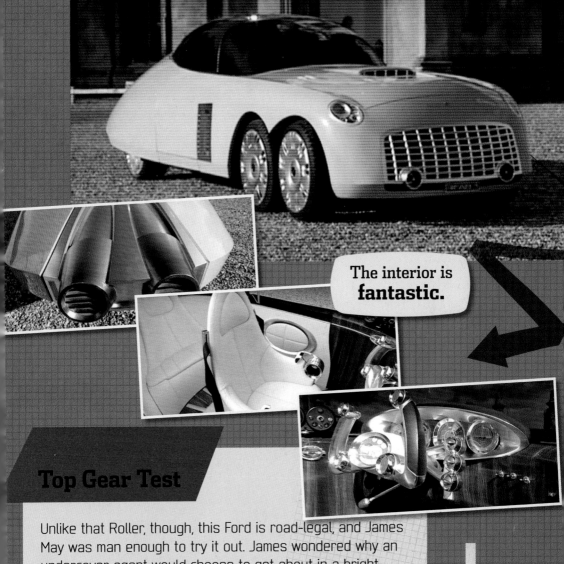

The interior is **fantastic.**

Top Gear Test

Unlike that Roller, though, this Ford is road-legal, and James May was man enough to try it out. James wondered why an undercover agent would choose to get about in a bright pink, 27ft-long car, but he loved the interior – all cream leather, chrome and shag-pile carpet. Unfortunately, this car turns heads better than it turns corners, thanks to it being 'the length of the average British village'. James was also disappointed to find out that, even though the car flew and floated in the film, it was all done with special effects: the FAB 1 doesn't really have a jet engine in the boot.

Why it's Mad

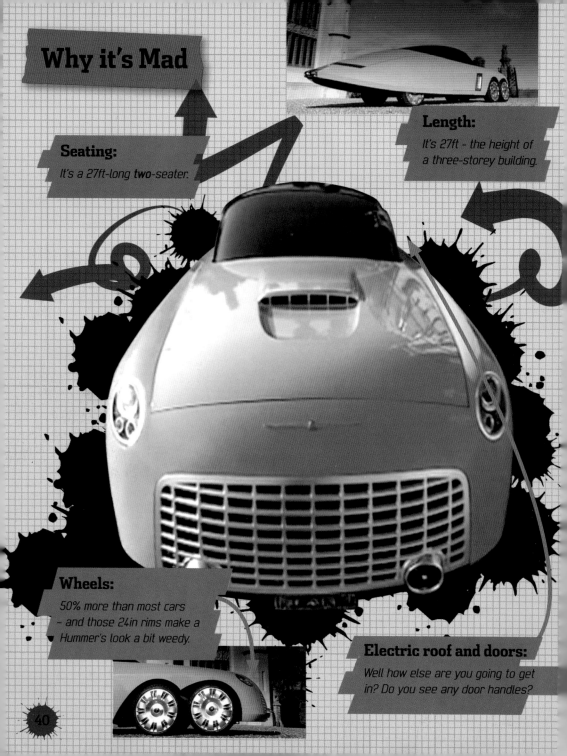

Seating:
It's a 27ft-long **two-seater**.

Length:
It's 27ft - the height of a three-storey building.

Wheels:
50% more than most cars – and those 24in rims make a Hummer's look a bit weedy.

Electric roof and doors:
Well how else are you going to get in? Do you see any door handles?

How to Use

1. Check the weather: there's a slight danger this film prop will dissolve in a rainstorm.
2. Be a rich and gorgeous girl, so that when you crash into someone (and it's bound to happen) you can charm them or bribe them and get away with it.
3. In fact, just get your chauffeur to take the wheel, sit back and enjoy the attention.

Steering it is like **helming** a **Spanish galleon.**

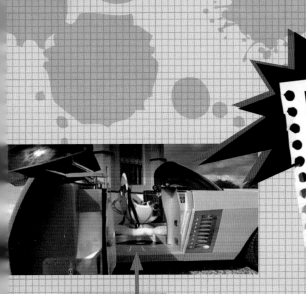

Interior:
Tasteful, eh?

Stats

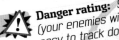

Engine: 7.4-litre V8

Everything else: classified

Danger rating: 9/10 (your enemies will find you easy to track down)

owler Wildc t

It looks like a Land Rover, only Land Rovers don't do 0-60mph in 4.8 seconds. Mind you, they don't cost £50,000 either. The body panels are fibreglass and the chassis is a spaceframe that takes three days to make. All of which creates a car that you could drive across Africa – very fast.

RRRRRR

This is **fast** in a **whole** new way.

Top Gear Test

Richard Hammond is a big Land Rover fan, so he loved driving the Bowler around an off-road track. You could barely wipe the smile (or all that grit) off his face. The Bowler took on any terrain he could throw at it. Then a professional rally driver took Richard for an even faster lap. He said he once dislodged a lung while driving it, thus proving that the driver will break before the Bowler does. On a separate test, the Bowler was raced by Ben Collins, another pro, against a champion all-terrain boarder at a downhill course in Wales. The boarder beat a Mitsubishi Group N rally car on the course – but he didn't beat the Bowler.

Why it's Mad

Spaceframe:
This thing's got more metal tubes than a cathedral organ. It's so strong, the car would support a 10-tonne weight on the roof.

Noise:
Looks like a 4x4, sounds like a racing car.

Interior:
What interior?

Spare tyres:
If you find these are in contact with the road, you've messed up big-time.

Load space:
A Land Rover hatchback! Designed for extra fuel tanks and a desert-racing water supply, not a sheepdog and a bale of hay. Takes up 370 litres of fuel.

How to Use

1. Buy a map of Africa and find Dakar on it.
2. Buy a dictionary and look up 'erg' in it (or check out this book's glossary).
3. Buy an atlas and stick a pin in it at a random point (but ideally on land).
4. Drive your Bowler Wildcat from this point to Dakar at high speed, taking in some ergs.

I am a driving God!

Stats

 Engine: Anything up to a 5-litre V8

Power: Up to 290bhp

 Top speed: 115mph

0-60mph: 4.8s

 Weight: 1825kg

 Top Gear lap time: 1m 39.4s (3.5-litre)

 Danger rating: 9/10

Carbon fibre – This is actually short for 'carbon fibre-reinforced plastic', since plain carbon fibre is just a cloth – a bit too floppy to build cars with. But by adding resin (plastic), you can mould it into just about any shape – such as the bodyshell of a supercar. It's lightweight and very, very strong.

Chassis – The structure that holds all the bits of a car together and provides its strength – like the frame of a bicycle. Cars used to be built by bolting the engine, suspension, body panels and everything else to a steel framework. These days, most cars don't have this separate frame; they use a monocoque body construction, which is stronger and lighter.

Downforce – The downward pressure on a car caused by the air flowing over it. By increasing downforce using wings and spoilers, designers can make racing cars stick to the track better – which means they can go round corners faster. But these wings create extra drag, which means the car isn't as fast on the straights.

Drag – Air resistance. Cars are measured by their 'drag coefficient', or Cd – the lower the Cd, the more slippery the car is through the air.

Erg – A dune sea: a large expanse of windswept sand dunes. You find ergs in the Sahara and other deserts, and organisers of rally-raids like to make competitors drive over them.

Forth Bridge – A famous railway bridge across the estuary of the River Forth in Scotland. Completed in 1890, it was the first bridge to be built of steel.

Girder – A strong beam, usually made of iron or steel, used in bridges and other structures designed to carry heavy loads.

Isle of Man – An island in the Irish Sea with a population of about 80,000 (and not just men). It's best known for the annual TT motorcycle race. The Isle of Man is sort of, but not quite, a part of Britain, since it has its own government and laws. For instance, most roads on the island don't have speed limits. It's got its own flag with a weird three-legged symbol on it, and the weird three-wheeled Peel cars were built there. But most Manx people have two legs and drive four-wheeled cars, like anybody else.

Le Mans – Le Mans (pronounced 'luh mon') is a city in northern France that's home to the famous 24-hour car race held in June every year. The 8½ mile-long race circuit outside the city includes the famous Mulsanne straight, where cars can reach well over 200mph. The race is a test of endurance – each car has three drivers who take turns behind the wheel. The winning Audi in 2008 completed 381 laps, covering 3226 miles at an average speed of 149.5mph.

Monocoque – A monocoque car relies on its body construction for its strength, rather than a heavy chassis frame. Think of the shell of a crab or the metal in a can of baked beans: neither is very thick, but they're surprisingly strong.

Prototype – An early, pre-production version of a new car.

Rally-raid – A long-distance off-road race for cars, trucks and motorcycles. Events usually take place over several days. Every day, competitors have to drive hundreds of bone-jarring, metal-bending miles over mud, rocks, sand and the wrecks of other competitors. The Paris-Dakar is the most famous rally-raid.

Rim – An alternative word for wheel, used by the sort of person who thinks it's cool to have blue illuminated windscreen washer jets.

Spaceframe – A very strong and fairly light chassis structure made up of lots of tubes welded together in a series of triangles.

Wheelspin – Pressing too hard on the accelerator can make a car's tyres lose their grip on the road. Then the wheels just spin instead of pushing the car forwards. Clues that this is happening include loud squealing noises, thick smoke, burning rubber smells and being overtaken by a milk float. 'Traction control' systems help stop it happening, but some supercars will spin their wheels in third or fourth gear, especially when the road's wet or Jeremy Clarkson is driving.

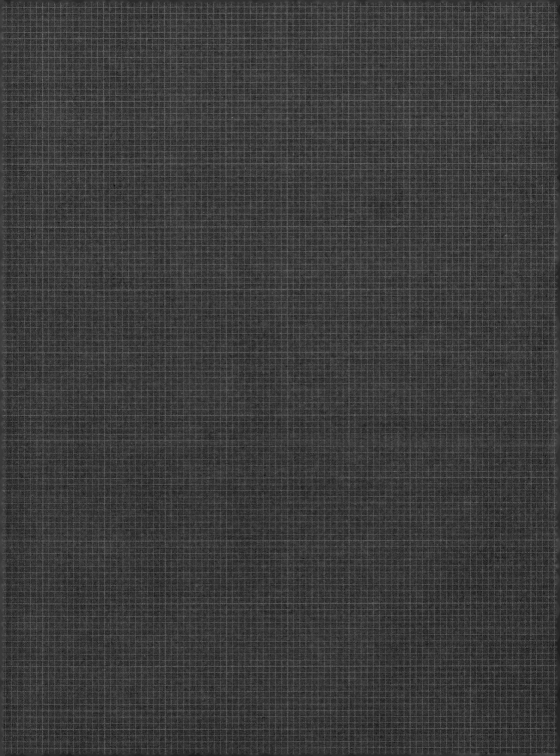